turn around,

BRXGHT XYXS

Rosebud Ben-Oni

GET
FRESHBOOKS

Get Fresh Books, LLC
PO Box 901
Union, New Jersey 07083

getfreshbooksllc.com

ISBN: 978-0-9989358-9-8
Library of Congress Control Number: 2019948486

Cover art: "Watchful" by Michael Hafftka
Cover font: "I tell you all my secrets" by Juha Korhonen
Cover & book design: Ann Davenport

Contents

For my beloved B,

now
&
always

turn around,

BRXGHT XYXS

Leave me the snake
It is the you before the screen while you are gone

—Olga Broumas

Matarose Tags G-Dragon on the 7

—after BIGBANG's "Fantastic Baby"

Matarose never comes home
She's hungry like a wolf
She's rosa de mota in lacroix
all the girls hail on queens boulevard
All the views she's killed
in the name of iman
& yasmin le bon
Mata's quite meta
Mata means kill
Rose a curve
from the real meat of it all
She's part my little pony
into bronies she has loved & loved not
by astro-pony
compatibility chart
She's the queerest part of me
What's left after the clubs close
& has yet to go
home she never goes when
she writes I always write
in bed just woofed down
a 3 musketeers   mata's on
a mission which is to say I'm
my most   queer my most mata-

    rose when she
        & I don't need all the girls
        in the yard

        don't need

all the girls in the yard
by which I mean
the one

who's not the one whose blocked
texts & torn up wish you wells
flicker still   That riddle
get you killed kind
          of a woman for whom
matarose almost cut off a foot
Went to the end of twobuck
ghosting rails
          My man is a little afraid
of mata   he accepts her tho
Lets her come & go
because I stay I am always
with him because mata
just wants every 7 train
to dissolve into g-dragon
sound wants you to howl

          boom mata mata

     boom mata mata

   wow

               g-mata dragonrose

The most pony of them all

                         g-mata7 dragontrainrose

   Don't wait up

          Never last stop never comes

                         boom mata mata

                              boom mata mata home

2

"Don't let yourself be hurt this time"

—Julee Cruise

"every now & then i get a little bit lonely"

before touching my face
kill the chickens
while i sleep

Dancing with Kiko on the Moon

On the far side we're kicking up tundra out of tú

& no one & no one

    on earth can see

        though they swear by
        (-we) though *do not sing to*
        moonwomen, sickle-hipped & shape

        -shifting & very well maybe & most certainly do

            their wishes bounce

        & chase after & chew

    our moondust

    when we are carousing with stellar winds & moon-

                gust

Oh moon we're over the you about you

Dear moon do you need a tundra to look after

    tú   dear familiar   dear shipwrecker

  salamander with wings of swallowtail

6

                    lucky charm fisher-

             queen waterless & aloof

It's just us two & we are twisters
that don't leave the ground to [   ]

Welcome to our moonhaus
& we don't have to ghost

shout— we're all the worlds living between tú
             which is why the moon

                              wears her sunglasses at night
                              where exploding stars fall
                              shock breakout bright

when kiko & I are kicking up
a tundra out of— tú
& summoning the sun & dew & oh

                    we're over ^{the you} of you

                              & howling until the wolves coo
                              until the cow jumps over [   ]
                              & we enchantress

             shine our super red from giants blue

        & dear nasa rogue
                 that's us collapsing
                        gravity so star power
                             we vogue

& oh meteorites & asteroids we set fire to

      & make more than a planet out of

dear [   ]

      & dear moon

         do you need a

do you need a

            she looks
                    after

      the far side of

   we are

all the dark side moonwalking after you

If Noah the Younger Sister

in an alternate universe like us
where we just wanna we just wanna
another is building
the last vessel
no more lemon trees
to carve our names
never the fortunate ones
we won't kneel
a slip of the tongue
reverses the world
oh girl
won't you too
unfurl
your most
bitch
kraken
real
it's not much to give up
a piece of tail
set the monsters free
and take their sails
we're still number one
and girls just wanna we just wanna

Odisea

The motorcycle I ride only turns left
When you go west I have to bear right
Such balance is not my forte
I'd rather bait
The wooden escalators at herald square
Until a stiletto sticks
I'm left to limp people think it's cute
When I'm playing them
When you're in berlin dancing in the street
Once I was a child facedown in the street
Thrown by a motorcycle that only turns left
A child who carries a knife
Is softened by
The kind who often gets away
We're the kind who often get away

In hong kong filled with rice wine and in-laws'
Hot pot I dance on their roof strewn
In orchids blue and green the kind of colors
You once said the ancient greeks couldn't see
Or didn't have the word for them
Perhaps it's not the blues I hear then
From this wine-dark south sea
When my phone tweets tweets it's you
Hang soon I'm in beijing
Let's meet wherever
Halfway might be
Half my shoes are gone
Got stuck when I was going up
The peak posting love to the future
I have left heels all over hong kong
In the most non-linear fashion

My bare feet only turn left
My arms and arms of egg tarts
Wrapped in leather scarves wine and grey
Darling why meet halfway let's go to mars
To cell towers in space and sing are you happy
With your service little miss purple rain
In the clouds let's rain down magic beans
Upon lotus-eaters who never know
Where they wake
Why tell them anyway
Tomorrow all the mallomars in space
Tomorrow all the mallomars in space
I too have been such foolish things
The one pouring champagne
For all the girls
Circling this world in jetskates
That only careen left
The night we are bobs and weaves
This night facedown in the street
Both merciless
And munificent so yes
Let's meet in medias res
The place no one thinks to name
Its shape like the great escape
Of steve mcqueen
Athena too will come
She's going all in for us
In this bike we trust
In these colors we sing
The gods from the machine

A Horse Dies Once That Is A Lie

Somewhere in kentucky she went for kicks
        spiked polka-dot mint
                julep *grade 1 stakes* white-gloved
                      clubhouse how-you-do-sees

until all the horses broke their legs & for all the horses my ex

                joined the seine-et-oise
            thoroughbred liberation front & she

    crashed all the bentleys & it was I who bled

in derby countryside where horses
        die in japanese
                slaughterhouses
                    defrocked
                          of rose blanket & blue ribbon

& how very they went
        in the kind of darkness knowing
                only my old
                      kentucky

home no longer a run for the roses it's besieged
    with cannibals & thieves
        & only millionaire's row sings

        a hero is a horse with a heart that never aches

          for lovers who cross them
          one too many times

when we kill one horse all of them die
waiting
long after kentucky & she
slips
white gloves on my hands
bent from carrying her on nyc streets
jammed
the wrong way in every direction

how merry are we

how merry

how bright-shine beaming no longer weeping
& she bears my head to the heat
& I let it all go
& bet my last hat & home
& how
& how very are we
& it changes everything

"every now & then i get a little bit lonely"

under wrought iron suns i clean the cages
strung upright by golden wire

plastic magpies perch on plastic branches
i kneel to wash their paint-chipped feet

she slumps over a large pit
knocking back bowls of menudo

is it getting late i ask
rust & firesales of fields
our eyes bright as xylene
lacing the soil

She Calls Once That Is A Lie

When she calls in the morning
I've changed my number address identifying features
I've sacrificed my name when she calls in the morning
With news she's selling my teeth on eBay
The teeth she broke off
One by one
While I was sleeping that is a lie when she
Calls in the morning I was awake
Each time she whittled away my ability to bite
Once on VH1 in a thrash metal rockumentary that is a lie
It was at the Kentucky Derby when she calls in the morning
She's taken all my hats and next my hair
& my scalp is an angry red gash
Once eating toffee by the sea that is a lie
When she calls in the morning it was a rest stop
In Jersey & the assortment was unreal
And of all things I chose Dentyne
Once I knew all the lemon drops by names
And identifying features they had names
When she calls in the morning she wants the children
When she calls in the morning & then the house
& the hospital where they won't operate on me
There are no spare parts not even a space between
Whistling
Like a fist of the bank in wet
Season lying through her teeth

Más Dolor

When you leave you go out a brick
        house
                stripped
                          of copper and sunbirds

At the high table I stand for the reckoning
I'm ready to sleep I'm ready to walk out
I need a big band   no   a badly written
                muse on roller skates
The winning hand of a musical
Oh evil woman of xanadu
To hell with your strange magic and mortal time
To hell with higgs boson and fading stars that guide
The stellar the loud the wide the look at me
The look at me in the night
                Wasted
      Wasted
Sister I wanna let it all hang out the dirty
dirty laundry the night our tongues spun
like some cirque du soleil
wheel of death
So   send in the pink ladies
No the spice girls no drown me in the pool

                        and darling I'll undivine
                        the dolphin within
                        every showgirl

        Cause when you leave

           I'll destroy

your memory

with a face
smothered
in cold cream
No   more   wire   hangers
in midnight raids
No basic instinct
to scratch my face
so I fall through a glass table
Let's just say when it happens
I'll know who killed me
I'm the good twin
surviving the strip club
when everything goes to seed
I was such a mean girl
so you never had to be
The shame has surfaced
The séance has ended
You are rubescent
in the sunrise of old man wishes
well I never got off the damn planet

Game over girl

game over

I'm already gone
                                        dismantling

            the junkyards

knocking the scrappers to their knees

        this time I'm going in   my sweet

                    sweet

                                            all day
    and all of the night

Self-Portrait as Golem

I don't go around leaving red curtains in ex-windows
If I wanna fight about it then only the secret rooms
Where I do not leave fingerprints I no longer have
Fingerprints I've left no trace
Behind those red curtains of rented rooms
I've cleared the cia customs and homeland
My hands no longer my hands but hummingbird
And faberge I've stolen the sunrise of monet
Pinned red feathers to the red chambers doors of thomas crown
And christian grey I have no feelings no lullabies to sing
When I poison them
Traded a nice pair of legs
For no blood no dna if I still had a heart
It would beat the beats of an earthquake
These days I don't need
To make a sound I'm pandemic
Appear as the red curtains that won't let you sleep
Weave knots into your back with songs of seabirds
Driving you into the sea it is not revenge
For the times you swore a blood oath
Under red moon and smoky redwood trees
And wished killer clowns from outer space on me
And all the lost souls and critters and trolls
Who I seized in my manos hands of fate
My many many wives I do not keep
Keep a picture of me above an altar of red wine and
Burning effigy the ashes not my ashes they chew in ecstasy
When the moon is full and werewolves
Cannot imprint on me I have cleared
Entire forests and doctor's orders and her majesty's
Secret service not even james bond can track me
Not the old red papers I do not collect

Worlds not enough where tomorrow will die
Waking on the red-eye
There by the wing all those nights you lost going
Back in time I am
All of them the eyes of steel bird
The red matter in the sky

"every now & then i get a little bit lonely"

losing face in the smoke
a mirage of some never
ending & winged

i cannot hear anything
over her quaking swing
she is a sluice
pulling apart patina

from grief she twists their necks

bloodied from eyes to short sleeves

Despite Their Best Efforts

I was little more
than a bottle cap of whiskey
More than once
I was rebozo slung
over a sleepy mouthed junkie
for CK one
Mira the everyday people baby
Mira like opening fire with candy
Mira my matted hair so model
off duty
While others donned tiaras
worldpeace and bikinis
I was sizing up
cops and clergy
At seven I ravaged a nativity
sullied
the feet of baby jesus
so he wouldn't be so trusting
Mira if we are the world
then I was a test of levees
I saw to it all my dolls
were waterboarded on a gurney
At dawn when they came home
exhausted from the double shift
another follower dozed in an ice bath
with one less kidney

     I was but the cliffhanger
from the great flood
babbling to a broken city
The future
crumbling bricks

and overcrowding
I am the first language
no one is speaking
Mira a different world
This is my blood and this
my body this time
you won't betray me
I am your kingdom come
the barricades
giving way mira even
the liquor stores are closing

If Cain the Younger Sister

My brother is a whitewashed synagogue.
His words are mud-bricked and windowless.
From desert frond and dust he builds a home.
A man of principle, my brother
Remembers the Alamo.
He tried to guide me
Training-wheel free
So I wouldn't fall
For men like Crockett or Koresh.
He promised I was a complete
Mensch and mother's family too,
Ofrenda of flower, skull and bread.
At ten he solved a dispute
By reciting Kaddish
On the Day of the Dead.
My brother would bury me if he had to.
My brother would build me a coffin
And nail it shut. To this day
He turns down the radio
Passing burial ground.
I never showed that kind of respect.
At sixteen I totaled his car
Outside Seguin
Looking for another city.
In the ER, mother screamed
And the nurse had no
Sympathy. I nearly
Killed a man.
I never confessed
I saw him coming
And careened
At full speed.

Never again
Will my brother sleep.
He locks the doors
And waits for me.
Every night tympani
Buried in the vistas
Awaken me. I emerge from
An ark covered in marigolds,
A feather child leaving her ossuary.
I died in the Indian laurels of San Agustín.
Brother I'd like to have said brother
You are the fort and I am the death wish,
Sacrificing all
At last stand.
Brother, the blood
On my hands. Brother,
You are the home and I am the wilderness.

Guns on the Table

In the years I lived
With a taiwanese former pop star
Who couldn't feed the business
Couldn't hang with the gangs of asia
Behind johnnie to's triad odes
In which there are no guns at all
In his films gangsters are strangled
They are chopped up in meat grinders
And fed to dogs
Tethered to sworn brothers
Who will stab to death sworn uncles
That's the business and could you
Could you
The former pop star's mother asked
She's produced films all over asia
She wants to know just what I'm made of
How would I handle
Would I go missing
For hours like carina lau
In *days of being wild*
Blindfolded
Shot topless
By those guns on the table
Could I could I too
Just to make a film would I
Sit in a restaurant straightforward
Somewhere in central
Where anyone who's anyone in hk knows
Business is done elsewhere
Would I write of mexico's guns
With hong kong gangsters
Who finance it all

Don't you know what I know
She said *when you roll up to the table*
What will you show

That summer 3 men came to my childhood home
Claiming they'd fix the cable
My parents didn't own
Then father wanted a gun but mama
Said no this woman
Loves clint eastwood and desperado
She forgives the scantily clad for the gore
My mama is guns on the table
Her first words in english
Were make my day no
At 12 while abuelo hunted javelina along the border
She chased away a man who came to take their home
She alone
With a butcher's knife
And then a shovel
After it all mama couldn't walk straighter
She threw off every saint and every novio
Don't forget she says *why el mariachi dies alone*

On the border police kidnapped an uncle
In that long before of mexico
Long before
When the cartels were still in colombia
They poked him in the ribs
Skinned a print off a finger
He was only freed when my family gathered
Enough cash the kind to bring
Guns to the table
And what of his grandson
The namesake of my abuelo
Born of the border
He got 60 years at 18
Gangs addiction first-degree because what else
What else but for guns on the table
I'm more like my cousin than you'll ever know
I'm no heroine
I'm not your girl

What would I do at times
To get done without the getting
When in israel I shot my first rifle
It knocked me off my feet   I was
A firehose of firemen thrown I arose
Vaguely heartbroken   then vengeful
I wanted more
Not some vato in his backyard
With tactic-issued alphabetized spit-polish
I wanted simple
Four shells pump action
Pick myself off
One by one
In some wide wide
Open   I wanted
Recoil   I WANTED
Recoil   I want
For my cousin
Strung on heroin
Making it known   through glass
Separating his hand from my own
At 18 he's done what he was to do
Now how to disappear
How to go
Without eating your heart
When someone rolling up to the table
About wolves and brotherhood

And what of a woman
What's she to do
When she knows the business
All too well when they came knocking
That summer knocking on the door
Honey little friend don't you know
K-dramas can't ever show
Anything at all even simulated
But in every one there's a woman
Seized by the arm don't you know
She wants to she wants to she has
To be told honey do you feel lucky
Well now don't you

{and you're never coming round}

she insists i wear sandals inside
side-eyes when i drink from the faucet
for wanting to savor the same bitterness
bottom-speckled as if
i've never known
anything else

Even Doves Have Pride

It's the straight girl I dated who's the most outraged
I married a man, who confessed behind curved hand
Just how much she hated
What I could give her again
And again. Back then I believed her. Truly.
Don't put me in a poem, she said, then read
One meant for another
And thanked me. *It takes a woman,* she guessed.
Or a genie. Perhaps the bottle only. *If I could live there*
Year-round and tax-free. Jump in. Death drop down
A fifth-floor walk-up. No wi-fi,
All pistols, crowded subway platforms.
Under Washington Square arch. Under Caravaggio
In Caffe Reggio. *Someone might* see us. I'd play rogue
Boyfriend assassin. I'm hard to keep
Alive. You'd think another woman
Would get this. In real life, I'm smaller than I appear
On screen. Whose screen. Wine by the crate.
Why aren't you saying anything, she'd cry
When I'd get the flu
Or talk about the future.
Dripping wax from flameless candles. Vanilla Maple
Turquoise Sky. I text single words. Random wireless
Popping up. Just paid for more data. I did no such thing.
I like a lot of photos on Instagram. Years later, she cries
Traitor. Executioner. Wet blanket. Sucking
All the power from the ballad.
But does she know what doves do
When they cry. When I've put them into a pot
And Snapchat a savage dinner. Rogue dove assassin.
Rogue genie assassin. Chapped-lipped,
Locust-limbed

And always cold.
Still the ticking
Of the *clock*, a hunger crooning
Under discount racks of returned clothing.
Thank God, she always fantasized my mother
Scooping me up, *you sound like the 2 pm set*
At a strip club. Girl not even. Years later, Mama gets a root
Canal and goes back to work. Same day. Same rogue waves
Mama passed on. Hard to keep alive. Red tide
First steps where pelicans
Eye small children in fair distance.
No exceptions. How in June algae blooms
Faucet to glass. 12-hour weekend shifts in a music store long
Gone, age 16. But straight girl wants live music. Crystal waters,
Silent bays. Take home more in a week than in a year I made.
Back then I believed her. Truly. I did no such thing.
She never heard a word, not the *ticking* into a dark
Screen, not the uncharged phone didn't mean
A world so cold didn't mean
It's— she was never
And neither
Was I
And I
Believed
No such thing
Never
Not even
The dryness of her eyes
When she cried
How do I get you alone tonight?

When I Roared It Sounded like an Accordion

That thing the mermaid tramples coming out of the sea
I am the squeezebox animal
Half-dead & beached
My neck of hashtag wounds
Drawn hastily
She thinks I'm heralding
Her first time on land
When I don't care if her new legs are lovely
When she tramples me I roar
The kind of octave
Running
Running off a cliff
On land my mermaid is what you'd call
On holiday in michael kors
Blends right into everything
Her thing is taking all the marmalade
& little plates & little knives
& pink whiskered wine
Her blood is antibiotics & ketamine
When we met I was again that thing
She trampled on a lovely sunday
Shooting gators in the everglades
When I roared she nearly shot me
When I roared sounding
I too could be a lady
If I wasn't drawn
So hastily
For that she picked me
She picked me
I am ashamed how happy
When I roar
& she takes

All the jam & cocaine & pats of butter
Off our plates
Until she is drowning
Drowning in all these things she longs for
We don't suspect a thing until she roars sounding
Can you see our unborn
Are feeding
When I roar don't worry
Only the strong will carry what eyes
Would have been what eyes when I roar
This is not your home anymore
I drag her back to the sea
When I roar I'm drowning
Only the strong
Won't sound
Like her anymore when I roar
They awaken in her drowned body
Rage against each other
Trample upon leg like leg
& bloodied fin

If Benyamin the Younger Sister

When I turn brundlefly I'm afraid my brothers
    will blow off my head

        perhaps they need
            insect politics
                not knowing adam
                    from marmalade

        Perhaps somewhere in a cave
        in an unmarked grave
        precious my precious
        Mother's last word
        my real name
        slept in
        no filter
        break
        the internet don't come for me brothers
        unless I hit send

              Make it rain

                        shameless
                            are insects
                                ever gone
                                      with the wind

            or between brothers
            do they break bread
            go batshit
            meth or get rich
            and die
            trying in insect coups seek
            asylum

pixie stix
carcass no you can't sit

with us you're missing a leg
          antennae
                    most of your head
                              your right hand

                    am I the first
                    last words
                    mother left
                    if I turn brundlefly
                    what of this never
                    name
                    corrosive enzyme
                    caught beneath a silver cup
                    mix it in
                    with your honey and milk
                    brothers I'll suckle
                    you dry
                    while mother's fasting
                    and I promise
                              nothing will you
                    stay then
                    when I turn brundlefly
                    when illness
                    is a form of possession
                    and all children
                    the original debt
                    a death to be
                    larger than desire

If Stripe the Younger Sister

I'm the who's who here's a commemorative
Keychain for all the doesn't she
Never eats a thing praise
Be who's inside
Every model
But a gremlin
& fast cars & dark
Theaters who butchers
Snow white no they shouldn't have fed us
After midnight congratulations here's a franklin mint
For getting in   who's
The hussy
My mogwai friend
Bedding the cartoonist who's the banker rolling in
His dirty boxers in the dumbwaiter after who pins
Takes aim at your lovely sad giz reputation
Your eternal sterling giz reputation
Side-eyeing
When we grind
Hands in the vitamix here's a lucky foot here's the original
Ideas who beheads the mother
Who feeds on the dog so who
Pupaes into I   the who
Of who's who   you & I
Before popcorn-crunching kids plucking
Plush you from shelves infinite
Before lifting the shades & our species
Disintegrates thanks to the who's who they say
The selfless the shared billy blankets this is why
I must break your arms & then your neck
Speeding in our little pink corvette
Into triple sun

By gelfling hand or else   by carol
Channing come together as the white queen
Gone sheep clark gable
A notch on the post of our stable we are starving
Boil the pet rabbit
My little tramp
We're not done yet
Call for the head of bambi another who's left
The matrix the glowing axe of optimus
Divine ultra magnus with broken
Static on the television who's who they ask
When we've taken who's that carol ann say it

{the best of all the years have gone by}

over on the island tap water
bleaches the fish
even in quick rinses
when i left the shorefront was sold
for next to nothing
but who even had that she
reminds me

All the Wild Beasts I Have Been

All the wild beasts I have been
Are ripping me apart again
I am a spiritual defector
In the time of
In the time of
I have a million excuses
I have failed
All those years I did not march
All those years I sprung
From some other head
From some other head
As some wild beast
As burning eyes
Of a chamseen
I burned the fields
I burned the wildflowers   suddenly
I prayed for forgiveness
Kicked the door in
All the doors in Jerusalem
Now uncles now aunts now cousins
Calling on my wedding day
Why   they ask   can't I understand
They will not under any law
Any sun
Any surfacing
Sanction my marriage
They are calling on my wedding day
For now there are riots on the streets
They live in the middle of things
And have never seen
It has never been a passing thing
The broken glass the sirens

Running   running
From rockets and blessing
And once I
Was all of this
I'd come out flailing limb
Explode
Like the eyes of a chamseen
Shelters shelters ducking
No it did not start with this
Kicking down the doors with this
In that BLACKOUT
and RAIDED and BROKEN when I was yes when I
Was all of this

          Now I am in repose in a Chinese dress
          My finger cast in the Song of Solomon
          The band cast in Hong Kong why
     Why are you calling
On my wedding day
Your voices your reasoning
When I was supine before the streets
Disloyal to the streets
I still chatter in the night while my love sleeps
I am feverish with
In the morning
In the morning
In our new york my love answers me
Knowing you will never speak
To him
He's just fine my love
Thinks grammar and spelling
Are beside the point
Eguana with an E is just as good
As the real thing
How will you pray   I ask   uncles aunts cousins
When your borders & walls fall
And all the beasts we've been
And all the beasts we've been
Call to the parted seas

To the tide rolling in
To the furthest white crest
What then
What of it all   drained
Taken of roar and limb you
Call then
                    to this other time

                        incorrect

                            some hours behind

                                with our fruit peels

                    hardening on the table

                        to this other other time

                where he and I he and I

                                    each day

                    surfacing

l u z

1. Spanish for "light"

2. According to Rabbinical legend,
the indestructible bone of the body,
the nucleus of the resurrection body.

This night is too long
Too long for a prayer do not go
Into that elsewhere I do not know
This woman next to you
Clutching a rosary
I recite the v'ahavta as she lights
Veladoras to saints I cannot name
The night is too long I've been awake
Too long to keep
Elsewhere   elsewhere now
Radios wrenches full-throttle the garage
All the cars you restored in the rgv and beyond
All the pickups bikes vans 10-4
My beloved
My mother is calling   to you it's late
It's not too late we have yet to inscribe
Your name on our doorposts and our gates
I have prayed before a ramshackle
Altar of 7 day candles
Back in queens   elsewhere
I cannot bring here
10-4 you kiss my childhood sidor and faded
Polaroids taken after I was born

Too early you'd said it was not too late
Over and over you'd said my name
I'd known all of you
Before I knew your name
This is not kaddish
This is not rain on shabbat
This is elsewhere
Inside a storefront church
I pray to milagros nailed on rotting walls
For years the night was too long
And we said next to nothing
Fed the mosquitos our blood
Rocking for hours on a porch swing
Now I can't get past
The bar and machinery of your bed
Half man half engine
Now I doubt
Now I'm asking
For saints I cannot
Name I bind as a sign upon your hand
This name on these doorposts
And on this gate now you are asking
The man I married to stay at your side
You ask for my rabbi
To marry your catholic son
You ask for my hand
Elsewhere now you ask for my hand only
At the bridge where the engine
Won't turn it's late they whisper
And kneel down to the floor
They kneel and pray
No
It's not too late
Crank it up
Pedal to the metal
My beloved
This road is not yet done
Tonight
Let's burn it up

Forgetting Is the Ghost That Keeps You Alive

I broke my key in a lock of an old home
I've never lived wanting it to be my own
Lately I'd rather wander the earth
Than ride to the end of the line I regret not
Missing my stop on buses in jerusalem
Because of borders on which I've lived
Because why can't she and why can't she
Live with whomever
Wherever I'm a little tired
More than that of all the hate
And all the hours I fought
The shuq closing on friday evening I forget
The sabbath no longer keep my key
Still broken
My husband has made copy after copy and puts post-its
On the front door yet I still forget
They are post-its I only see tangerine
And lime green I forgot to tell you
They taste like nothing nor do they bloom
And fly out of crumpled cocoon I forgot to tell you
I am less and less hungry
These days it's always something
Crushing my insides with songs of revenge
And worry that I want to bleed for everything
That I sometimes do and I forgot to tell you
The trees I still cannot name on skillman avenue
Weep for the butterflies that will never be
I forgot to tell you that I ate just enough death
By chocolate to have said I'd ate the whole damn thing
That for days I was last seen
Circling
All of the trees in queens in the furthest reaches

Of queens that for every million ovals
A perfect ring
For a planet that perhaps
Needed me I forgot to tell you my dear friend
That I love you after you said it to me
How it rang true
And rang past me to this world
This world not only

Axolotls Do It Better So Now I Am an Axolotl

Not all goodbyes are tragic unless they begin
for someone else & this one did & I can't stop

      carrying you under my coastal grooves
         where there's a hundred years
          of you

          larval for life, forever newt-
          like & never
          to arise the canals
          & floating gardens.

          Go on & feed

          [finite[them]] to kelp & coral reefs.

          Never again to such perfect day
          security would I promise our tartare
          lives. Or would I try to close such eyes

          that bury me
             alive in sea anemones growing toward
               our feet & never where the sun
                  would be

     do we bite off each other's limbs
     & return in angles un-right

         when our ancestors said no
           & went back in,
             supercluster that would
               drown the universe.

We are the layer under human skin.

We are swimming toward each other
      under their dead skin
      like a thousand holy grails
      smashed
      against
      white cells & terrain
      graces. My darling laurel
      -wreathed
      & unripened,

                there is only you

      knocking down
      a sad plastic fish bowl tower
      with melting stone
      & dandelion.

{and giving off sparks}

amazons on open t-stands cock an eye
flatten to unease

go ahead she sings rewashing the dishes
when i flip

the vacuum switch, shuttered maquilas
bad soil &

sicarios in training fill the room
they puff up

& scream— she laughs deeply from drainpipes
a love bare-

footed
& beyond censor

Shitty Little Dinosaurs

There are birds arising in these flying little dinosaurs

There might be two or three in a single little cannibal

who steals
the last piece of chicken
though we lay out premium seed
every night
& every morning
on the rooftop of my in-laws
where my husband & I sleep
in a little room
in a little bed
with its little canopy
of red ribbons
& mosquito netting

Every night we watch them
like beasts awakening
in cave paintings
without belief
in anything
but themselves these
flying little creeps
who seem to know it all
who don't listen to god
or natural law
Without fear they remain
forever
not dying
outside a promise
land no they enter wherever

however chewing through wood
& rag & screen

    & when the clouds lay low in the afternoon
    from the haze come dragons too
    who descend to undo
    clothespins & nails loose
    At least five little dragons in each
    whose true fire is their speech
    taken from everyone
    & everything
    Muffled laugh track & hawk shrill
    quarreling lovers
    & siren
    church bells
    In august drench until the sky dims
    the whole of hong kong screams out of them
    They taunt & torment & yet
    we never hear them coming
    & they are never of one place
    these shitty little things
    who won't leave a single grape
    to roll lonely
    on my plate
    because once they were cockatoos
    in shitty little crates
    crossing the south china sea this
    they have not forgotten

        Every night they feel the need to escape
        to not not arise from our skylines
        while I hide
        my most precious things
        as if they will always be with me
        as if the day will come they do not
        return to the rooftop
        where I'm not holding my breath
        face pressed
        against torn-up mesh

        What they are this earth never left

I see the sunrise & sunset within seconds
                                        there are

hundreds & hundreds of birds arising within every one of them

{turn around}

until the claws can't be pulled back in

until we beckon all the coyotes to the crowded streets

until all the coyotes are city limits
        prowling like queens & can't
                you love {that} what i am
                        can't be pulled back ever
                                again {turn around}

                        there's no saying when

     i am a gila monster carrying away
           a{nother} golden girl in gold lamé

               into sunsets blistering
                      with daffodils & supple
                    decay

     until our mouths are so full I can't tell you
          all we can beget is poison
                 & it's the most joyous
                      of joyful things

          until we shut down every single
          waffle house
          & like tornados
          & scatter
          smother & cover
          our own hideouts in bones
          & hashbrowns
          & nothing again is open
          24 hours & there's nothing

we cannot take to {   the end of the line }

    turn around

  until you've had it
with trying to iron out my pucker
& frown

        until all my love only in dark & all of the time
        until chew & chew
        into broth & rubber burning through
        until giving off spark our xyxs
        until I can't turn brxght
        brxght
        without turning
        into
        nothing i can say
        oh even forever has no place
        in our time
        for *you*
        for {x} *I* {x}
        oh say right now forever has to die

If Delilah the Younger Sister

You say peace won't come from one person
Or poems it isn't
Wildflowers and plowing wilderness
No it wouldn't come if we let it
Piety isn't a bright blue sky but its absence
The other side the same
Seven days and seven nights you say grinding
In the prison house no where do we go

                    Where do we go now
                        Where do we go

String skipping I'm making faces
With j michael martinez   conjuring
The good accidents the wrong times those glam
In the grunge era
                        Where we exit
            Sheena headlines
The ramones   catch it on j michael late night
Arsenio there's a revival kip winger headlines twisted sister
Skipping rope on torn j michael
Halos there's a revival my dear dear dead ones hanging out
In the roadhouse is that you samson here's one last fight
Sweep the leg ehud the left-handed BE NICE until it's time
Kiss
My
Converse and gideon
Pluck from your bowl and wool this

            I I I I I

Reborn a mercedes on feeder roads   I'm the big man
Filling vacancy I've possessed patrick swayze
Shaved heads and brass fettered the monster
Trucks driven to this j michael
Eat world where all the boys and girls
Belong to a j mötley michael crüe
The last tour last exit to the wake   raving raving
Where do we go where do we go now

Sweet

Marilyn j michael manson of mine yes
Drunk in heart-shaped burlesque yes
The mosh pit oh the accidents
A cracked skull a copped feel fickle hands
Carrying us off   if not a busted strobe
If not a ring-ripped nose   if cracked
Concrete beneath now where do we go
The hills are alive with michael van
J halen where do we go now
The rattail in hand
Whipping
Motorcycle
Wind

Stepping Away with Diego Baez

If this is not Latinidad then no we are not
Post-pulling prompts from a hat
I'd like to take a nap but now Diego's asking
Us about summer with our eyes closed I don't get that
My eyes never close Diego I'm sick of beach umbrellas
And flamingos it's hard to speak about Jerusalem
When I just want to love like XO why are we
Always looking back and pulling pacts out of hats
If that is not Levantine then no I'm not
Poems in which lemon drops ruin me
I hunted for trolls in evergreen
Around 1:10 or so because Lorna Dee says
To remember Diego I am the fist of the bank
And it's not a competition but I'm getting married
Too and summer with my eyes closed is my husband
Who wants us to be a single room
To stop answering calls at 3 am from family in Jerusalem
Telling me it's the end all over again that's why I woke up like this
I woke up like this looking
Post-Oslo
Post-accords one and two to be sure it's not you Diego
Or the flamingos so divine on the lawns with stone angels
It's not PTSD anymore than post-Ricky Martin
Menudo I like riding around with you and Juan and Octavio
And Darrel Alejandro too post hollering at the wolves
Post strange ghosts in elevators asking after summatime
Like it's for the asking
If not for our eyes only then no now why
Why would they ever close

I Guess We'll Have to Be Secretly in Love with Each Other & Leave It at That

To can't do. To overly over-you,

      to te amo [wrong name], to songs of wronged
              I think we & planting boxwood & snowdrop

                        for not our winter
                        children, nor sweet box
                        or winterberry.

              To facetiming winter silence

for hours. To no camellias & christmas rose touching through a screen

                    & still not sorry

about "somehorse"
      I knew

      in iceland for less than a week

         & some other life lurking
           on black sand shores.

           To my life, to yours,

      to sulking

under half-sunken moons & oh the places we won't go,

         to not airbnbing
            haciendas of airy
               rooms & canopy beds
                  engraved with lions

rose-tailed

& rose-maned.

To drug restaurants
that serve only cobra lilies
with a side of blackbirds
who wield spiked hammers—

a kind of punishment

for that]]horse[[I still long for.
To splinters & spitting
the names I'll never
curse you

in kitchen inferno [when burning certain animals]
without remorse. To your most exquisite
stews & fermented
cabbage jars
I won't break

rushing

to catch a broken down train.
To that first trail we missed.
To falling off & eroded hoofprint.

To the city you saved

by sticking a scorched trainer

in sliding door &

what's so wrong

with hell anyway. To

happiness
as a betrayal of what is happening
to people we love
& to people not just waiting around to die.
To love as resistance but not always

the way back. To I can't can't I. To you

crashing into the bathroom
    & fishing me out of the sink
        & carrying me in your arms

like that scene in the bodyguard
    only the song I sing has no queen,
        has no eyes
            or dreams, there is only
                dim & dog-eared
                    kaddish. To forgiving me

for all the plums I'd most certainly devour.
    To the platypus & fisher king, to breaking
        in case of emergency.
        To reading adonis

                in a crowded bar while televisions
                    signal flare amid a canopy
                    of crows.

                To having hope
            in our pop-up whit of the world,
        its edges sour & peeling.

To never having really left jerusalem
    which is why I'm still busted stars
        & throwing elbows.

To the hours we made horses between nightfall
    & war. To should go home. To leaving it
        the longest way
            of derailed horsecry
                & amaranthine bones.

Acknowledgments & Notes

Grateful acknowledgment is made to the editors of the following journals in which these poems first appeared, some in different form or with different titles: *The Adroit Journal, The American Poetry Review, Best American Poetry Blog, B O D Y, Dialogist, diode, glitterMOB, Hyperallergic, Luna Luna Magazine, Matter: A Journal of Political Poetry and Commentary, Nepantla. Poetry, Prelude, Sinking City, So to Speak Journal, TriQuarterly, Tinderbox, TYPO, Underblong* & *The Volta.*

Infinite 7 Train Love to my one & only Brian who makes me believe in tomorrow.

So much gratitude for CantoMundo, The New York Foundation for the Arts (NYFA) for fellowships that supported the creation of this book & a thousand brilliant stars to shine upon the entire Get Fresh team, especially Roberto Carlos Garcia who saved this book.

Still madly in love with the trifecta that is Bakar, Robin & Cheri.

To the poetic & artistic multiverse to whom I've forever tethered: J. Michael Martinez, Darrel Alejandro Holnes, Ruben Quesada, Gabby Bellot, Diane Chang, Holly Burdorff, Grisel Acosta, Vincent Toro, Jason Koo, Carolina Ebeid, Becca Klaver, Nomi Stone and Michael Hafftka, all of whom saw these poems early on. Grateful for you.

Much love to the family, especially to my parents and my husband's parents; to James, Josey & Andrew; to Stacey, Mike "The DMG," George & Meredith. In memory of my late Uncle Balani & Aunt Oliva. Abrazos to Ben (whose jokes are still just kinda funny), Julie & Rachel. For all aunts & uncles & cousins in the RGV, Chula Vista, Toronto, Hong Kong & elsewhere.

Aimee & Scott forever. & their sons Jackson & Hunter. & Teddy & Baxter. Still missing Rocky.

To Jenny Kaminsky for showing up when it counted. (& spinning my mama around on the dance floor on Padre.) To Menelle Sebastian for being one of the most amazing people I know.

A lot of the conversation that made this book what is took place over many wonderful meals at Tim Chen's Quaint on Skillman Avenue in Sunnyside, Queens. Tim, like his restaurant, is one of a kind.

"Odisea" is for Darrel Alejandro Holnes.

"Luz" is written in living & loving memory of my Uncle Julian "Balani" Gomez the II.

"Forgetting Is the Ghost That Keeps You Alive" is for Ruben Quesada.

"{turn around}" is for Danielle Pafunda.

"If Delilah the Younger Sister" is for J. Michael Martinez.

About the Author

Rosebud Ben-Oni is the winner of the 2019 Alice James Award for *If This Is the Age We End Discovery*, forthcoming in 2021. She is a recipient of fellowships from the New York Foundation for the Arts (NYFA) and CantoMundo. Her work appears in *POETRY*, *The American Poetry Review*, *POETS.org*, *The Poetry Review (UK)*, *Tin House*, *Guernica*, *Black Warrior Review*, *Prairie Schooner*, *Electric Literature's Recommended Reading*, *TriQuarterly*, *Hayden's Ferry Review*, *The Journal*, *Hunger Mountain*, *The Adroit Journal*, *The Southeast Review*, *North American Review*, *Salamander*, *Poetry Northwest*, among others. Her poem "Poet Wrestling with Angels in the Dark" was commissioned by the National September 11 Memorial & Museum in New York City, and published by *The Kenyon Review Online*. Her second collection of poems, *turn around, BRXGHT XYXS*, is being published by Get Fresh Books in 2019. She writes for *The Kenyon Review* blog, and is currently editing a special chemistry poetry portfolio for *Pleiades*, and is finishing a series called The Atomic Sonnets, in honor of the Periodic Table's 150th Birthday. Find her at 7TrainLove.org